Be Prepared, We Are All Going to Die

Be Prepared, We Are All Going to Die

Life Lessons I Learned along My Journey While Caring for My Sick Loved Ones

B. Jane Jones

BOOKLOGIX
Alpharetta, Georgia

Although the author and publisher have made every effort to ensure that the information in this book was correct at the time of first publication, the author and publisher do not assume and hereby disclaim any liability to any party for any loss, damage, or disruption caused by errors or omissions, whether such errors or omissions result from negligence, accident, or any other cause.

Copyright © 2023 by B. Jane Jones, LLC

All rights reserved. No part of this book may be reproduced or transmitted in any form or by any means, electronic or mechanical, including photocopying, recording, or any information storage and retrieval system, without permission in writing from the author.

ISBN: 978-1-6653-0609-6 - Paperback
eISBN: 978-1-6653-0610-2 - ePub

These ISBNs are the property of BookLogix for the express purpose of sales and distribution of this title. The content of this book is the property of the copyright holder only. BookLogix does not hold any ownership of the content of this book and is not liable in any way for the materials contained within. The views and opinions expressed in this book are the property of the Author/Copyright holder, and do not necessarily reflect those of BookLogix.

Library of Congress Control Number: 2023905049

⊚This paper meets the requirements of ANSI/NISO Z39.48-1992 (Permanence of Paper)

0 4 0 3 2 3

To Roy, my loving husband for over fifty-two years. For all the loving memories, good times and bad, and the many lessons we learned along the way. Thank you for everything.

Above all to my Lord and Savior Jesus Christ, who we couldn't have survived the good and the bad times without.
He is with us always.

Contents

Introduction ix

Chapter 1
Car Insurance 1
Chapter 2
Renters or Homeowners Insurance 3
Chapter 3
Health Insurance 5
Chapter 4
Cancer Insurance 9
Chapter 5
Life Insurance 13
Chapter 6
Travel Insurance 17
Chapter 7
Short-Term and Long-Term Disability Insurance 19
Chapter 8
Long-Term Care Insurance 21
Chapter 9
Wills 31
Chapter 10
Trusts 37
Chapter 11
401(k), Annuity, and IRAs 39
Chapter 12
Prearrangements, Funeral or Cremation, Plots and Headstones 43
Chapter 13
Things to Do after Your Loved One Passes Away 49
Chapter 14
The Final Chapter (The New You) 55

Letter From the Author 59
Appendix 61
Acknowledgments 67

Introduction

Be prepared, we are all going to die.

Until then we all need to be prepared to hopefully take some of the burdens off our loved ones. When that time comes, it is a matter of *when*, *where*, and *how* that might occur, either suddenly or after a long illness. Accidents and disasters happen every day—all of that is in God's hands.

This is my story documenting the things I was able to do and wasn't able to do before and after my loved one passed away.

I am afraid that I have learned a lot about being prepared by discovering I was *not* prepared. The hard times teach us a lot, if only we learn from them. I will tell you upfront that I am not a lawyer, CPA, or insurance agent. But I hope this book helps someone and that they won't have to go through what I did. Parents can try to tell you what to do but we don't always listen until years later. Then you might say, "I wish I had listened to them sooner."

This is my story of what I have learned after dealing with a lot of different situations in my life.

It was over thirty years ago when my sister and I lost our dad. Our mother and dad were divorced, and Mother had remarried someone else. Because of this, it was up to us to make all the decisions for our dad, who had a massive stroke and nearly died. The doctors told us to decide on three things: where he was going to live, who would take care of him, and where he was going to be buried. We also had to decide whether to sign a DNR ("do not resuscitate") order for him. He was in his early eighties, and we knew he would not want to be on a machine for the rest of his life. So, we signed it. We decided to put him in a nursing home, where he got better and lived for over eight more years.

During this time, Daddy was somehow named in a class-action lawsuit and was given a check. We knew he was not going to be around for long, so my sister, Lane, and I went to the funeral home and made prearrangements for him, using this money as a deposit.

He died the day before he would have been ninety-one.

It has now been over five years since we lost our mother. Three years before that we lost our stepfather. After Dad died, I said that I would, hopefully, never get caught unprepared again. So, I made an arrangement to prepay on our stepfather. Mother signed all the paperwork and I made the payments each month on that. After he passed away, my sister and I set up prearrangements to prepay for Mother. At this time, she was in the early stage of Alzheimer's. We then had to put her in a nursing home.

During this time of dealing with Mother and our stepfather, Lane and I were also dealing with our husbands' declining health. Her husband has COPD. Mine had congestive heart failure, diabetes, kidney disease, and later, cancer. After almost losing my husband, Roy, the first time from diverticulitis—he nearly bled to death—I made up my mind to go and do the prearrangements for both of us. Thank goodness I had already made and paid for a lot of things at the time of his death.

But you are never prepared for all that happens after you say good-bye to your loved one. This is why I am writing this book: to inform people to be better prepared and hopefully have some things paid for in advance. If not for you, do it for your parents, your children, maybe even your grandchildren and great-grandchildren.

Until you experience this, you don't really know everything you will have to do. I thought I had everything lined up and it would be no big headache. Boy, was I wrong. It had been a long time since our dad, stepfather, and mother had died. In those years, a lot was different. But laws changed, especially after the pandemic hit. Some things changed for the better, and some, not so much. But you just deal with what is happening at that time and place.

Chapter 1

Car Insurance

Let's start at the beginning: making plans with your car insurance.

Basically, if you own a car or other kind of vehicle (boat, motorcycle, ATV, etc.), you need insurance on it for your protection as well as your passengers and others on the road. Your parents may have been paying for this until you got out of school and on your own. So, you may not even realize this is important insurance you will need. You can shop around and get cheap insurance but be aware of what it may or may not pay for. You get what you pay for. Find an insurance company that you feel comfortable with. You could have insurance with them for the rest of your life.

We were with one insurance company for years while the kids were growing up. When you have teenagers, and especially boys, the rates go way up when they start to drive. You may have to sign that they will only drive certain cars. We did. Boy, was that a hassle. But you do what you have to do.

I got to check around at other companies. My husband's friend told him to check out the company he was with, so I did. We have been with them for a long time

B. Jane Jones

now. They are friendly and you always get to talk to a real person. All we ever have to do is call them and they will help with whatever the situation is, whether it be broken windows, down trees on the fence in the backyard, etc. Even when I had an accident years ago, they took care of things. The other person did not have insurance. Luckily, our insurance had protection for that. Thank goodness it was only car damage and no one was hurt.

Get the best insurance you can with a good and honest company.

Chapter 2

Renters or Homeowners Insurance

By now, you are probably finished with school and out on your own. You're probably renting an apartment for the first time. My sister, Lane, and I rented an apartment together after we graduated high school. At this phase of our life, we were furnishing our apartment with hand-me-down furniture and yard-sale items. Hopefully, you are able to get renters insurance with the company you have your car insurance with. We, unfortunately, did not get renters insurance. I don't even remember if we knew that kind of insurance existed, let alone that we needed it.

When Roy and I got married, we rented a house from Roy's grandfather, which we did for a few years. During that time, we were able to get renters insurance with the company we had our car insurance with. Luckily, we never had to use it, but it was a small price to pay if we had needed it. Some companies give discounts when you bundle your car and home together.

When the kids were out on their own, we were finally able to buy a house. We got home insurance with the company we had all of our other personal insurance with. At the closing, the surveyor said we had to get flood insurance on the house simply because it was located in a flood plain. We had no idea this was the case until we were signing all the papers. Roy was ready to walk out. He looked at me and said, "If you want the house then handle this."

So, I did.

I called our agent from right there in the room in front of the lawyers and all. Tim, our agent, laughed and told me he would sell us the flood insurance for $200 a year, but he was surprised we needed it since the house sat about one hundred yards up the hill from the road. Tim said that was the easiest he has ever sold insurance.

Luckily, we never had to claim anything on the flood insurance. After about twenty years of paying flood insurance, the county did another survey and took our property out of the flood plain, and we were able to cancel that insurance. The next year after we canceled, there was a five-hundred-year flood that missed us by about a quarter mile. We were a little worried during that weekend rainstorm. A lot of people lost their homes, and businesses were underwater, but luckily for us, the flooding never got to us.

There are choices you have to make in life and that was one we hoped would not come back to haunt us. Luckily, it didn't.

Chapter 3

Health Insurance

Everyone needs health insurance. Your parents probably covered your insurance until you turned twenty-six. After that, you are on your own.

When Roy and I got married, he did not get health insurance for me through his job, at first. That was a big mistake. Like I said, I learned the hard way about some things, but I learned from those mistakes and the lack of judgment at the time. After nine months of married bliss, I got pregnant. Without insurance, we had to pay out of pocket for each doctor's visit and medicine.

We didn't know the baby was going to be a boy. This was before ultrasound helped you find out the sex of the baby. For some reason, I had to take medicine so I would be able to carry our son full term. I don't remember why, now, since that was over fifty years ago. That was hard, but we managed the extra expense. When our son was born, he was healthy and had no complications. Roy had to take out a loan to pay the hospital bill. This was before they would let you make payments. Roy said he thought about telling them to just keep me and my son since they wouldn't take payments. But now we had to get the loan paid off. We did.

Roy made sure we had health insurance for all of us after our son was born. Live and learn. So, we had insurance when our daughter was born three years later. What a relief it was having that insurance. This was at a time when most companies paid all or at least part of your health insurance monthly premium.

You need to be aware of what your health insurance's maximum out-of-pocket total is for each year. Some do not have a maximum and some are at one million a year.

We were very lucky and got in with a good insurance company and stayed with them for over fifty years, and still counting. We had some troubles with them, sure. You have to learn the way the insurance company handles things like claims and claim disputes if they arise—and they did. I remember one time we had to rush Roy to the ER. He nearly bled to death. Our insurance said to take him to the nearest ER, which I did. I asked the nurses at one point if all of these charges cleared through our insurance, and they said yes.

Well, after a week's stay in the intensive care unit, he was released. We later got a bill from the hospital stating we owed over $16,000 that the insurance did not cover. I was really upset. We didn't have that kind of money. They said they would turn us over to a collection agency. Then I was even more upset. I had been calling the insurance company about this and getting the runaround. They said the bill was paid. I said if a bill has a dollar amount still due it is not totally paid. They said they paid their part. I got the address to file a dispute on the bill. I sent a letter stating my objections to them not paying the entire bill. Especially when they said to go to the nearest ER. Well, it took six months of phone calls but they finally sent Roy a check for the amount not paid to the hospital. So, he deposited that and then wrote a check to the hospital.

Another time, I had to call 911 to have Roy carried to the hospital. This time, I knew to have the ambulance service transport him to the insurance company's preferred hospital. They did. Later, I got a bill from the ambulance service stating we owed over $1,000 that the insurance company did not pay for. So, I wrote a letter to dispute the bill with our insurance company. I found out that the ambulance service was not a *preferred* ambulance service under contract with our insurance company. I told them that when I had to call 911, I did not know they had a contract with a certain service and I didn't have time to shop around. And that they should let people know about this before they needed help. I also said I would report them to the insurance commissioner if this wasn't settled. This bill came in after Roy had passed away. I also told them I was going to turn it over to our lawyer if this wasn't paid in one month. The day before I had an appointment with the lawyer, they called and said they had sent a check directly to the ambulance service.

There are always ways to dispute a claim. If you have a question, don't just pay the bills as they come in. Make sure you really have to pay the amount they are stating you owe.

Even if you have a job and they are covering you with

one insurance company, down the line they may find it to their benefit to change companies. We had that happen at least once. It was probably due to the rising costs of the insurance and the number of participants in their plan. All of this is out of your control. Again, be aware of how this insurance company handles things. No two insurance companies are alike. When an employer changes insurance companies, you have a choice to go with that company with the rate they are going to charge or to shop to see if you can get coverage on your own. Now, a lot of companies don't even offer that coverage for employees.

I know when you are young you think you will live forever and nothing will happen to you. Been there and done that. But *be prepared*. We are all going to get sick with something at some point. We are only human. We are not invincible. The older you get, the more prone to illness, disease, or accidents you are. That is when it is harder and more expensive to get insurance.

You need to have health insurance to cover your wellness checkups each year. Women should have mammograms each year after a certain age. Men need to be checked for prostate cancer every so often. You need a colonoscopy to screen for colon cancer every five and ten years after a certain age. This way, if you do have an illness, maybe you can catch it early. Insurance companies vary on when they will start covering the costs of these tests. There are some hospitals and clinics that do these tests for free if you qualify. You can check the web to see if you can qualify for this and where they are located.

Chapter 4

Cancer Insurance

In this day and time, it would be wise to get cancer insurance—kids get cancer, and older people get cancer.

I learned about this type of insurance from my mother not many years after I had married. Luckily, my mother and stepfather had this insurance when he got lung cancer. Their policy paid an upfront amount when first diagnosed. They put that amount up to help pay for what the insurance did not cover. After they got that amount, they had to file claims on all the treatments and medicine. It paid a certain percentage on each bill. Believe me, it could have been financial ruin for them if they did not have this policy.

Along with cancer insurance, you need to be aware of what your loved one is going through during this difficult time and take into account their ability of driving themselves to appointments or not. There are hard decisions you might have to make, for their safety as well as others. My mother had given up driving years before my stepfather got cancer, so he drove himself to radiation treatments every day for about six weeks. When I would come to visit them, he always wanted to drive. I knew this was not what should be happening at this point. But to keep the peace, he would drive. Lane and I had a discussion on how to stop him from driving because we knew it wasn't safe for him to do so. That was solved before we had to make that decision. He drove to the store one day and the police brought him home and told Mother they didn't want to see him on the road again. He didn't have his glasses, but he would never tell anyone what happened and Mother wasn't told either. So, she took the keys from the police, hid them in a desk drawer, and told him that I had them. He only asked me once about it and I told him we would get whatever they needed.

I believe this insurance is also based on your age and health at the time you purchase it. The sooner you buy it, the cheaper it is. For some policies, this insurance is not too expensive, and the premiums never go up. I bought this when we were young and thank goodness I did. At age sixty-five, in the state of Georgia, you have to change to a fixed dollar amount instead of the "pay as you go" claim. I changed ours to a dollar figure that was based on the premium I had been paying on the previous policy. When Roy was diagnosed with colon cancer, he sent in the biopsy report and cashed in his policy. After he cashed his policy in, Roy then said because he didn't know if he would survive the chemo and surgery, he wanted a new truck before he died. So, he put a down payment on one. You need to listen to what your loved one is saying or wishing for because you never know if this might be their last wish. It was for Roy. He died four years after that.

Luckily, we had good insurance with his retirement

benefits. When he started going for all the cancer treatments, I kept an excel sheet on all the charges, what the insurance paid, and what we had to pay. It was staggering. I stopped after it went over a half million dollars the first year. We went out of network for the cancer surgeon. Never did get a bill on that one so I don't know what that costs, but my guess would be quite a bit. We kept having to pay the deductibles each year and the co-pays.

I am glad we got our doctor to operate. He specialized in colon cancer, and we liked him from the first meeting. He was honest with us. Roy asked him what would happen if he didn't have the surgery and the doctor said he'd have a year or less to live and the end would not be easy. So, he decided to have the surgery. I think that gave him four extra years with us. You need to find a doctor that will answer all of your questions so you can make an informed decision that is good for you.

Roy was good about going to get his six-month CT scan to make sure the cancer was not back after the treatments and surgery for the first year. Then he had a really bad fall after his surgery. He refused to see a doctor for two years. When they did the scan, they found one of his vertebrae was crushed. By this time, he was in a lot of pain. The doctor told him since it had been over a year, there was nothing they could do. They would not even give him pain pills for this. Roy then refused to go for another scan after that. We will never know if the cancer had come back or not. He lived in pain for the last two years. If he only had the scans every six months then maybe they would have been able to do more for him. He was so stubborn at times.

At one point, he told me and the kids I was the reason he was still alive. I would be the one to stress to the doctors and nurses about what his care should be, and on occasion, they would give him some pain medicine. When you are going through cancer or any major health issues, you do need an advocate that will stand up for you and get you the best care that is out there with the insurance you have.

Even if you have insurance, a local cancer group can help you with some of the out-of-pocket expenses you still have to pay. Since Roy had to go every day for six weeks for radiation trips, I was able to get free gas cards that helped pay for some of that cost. Not all, but every bit helps. If a loved one of yours is diagnosed with cancer, check with your local chapter to see if you qualify for any help. They offer gas, lodging, and transportation to treatments. Unfortunately, we were not at a location that could provide the transportation. It doesn't cost anything to talk to them, and you might be able to get some help.

Chapter 5

Life Insurance

This was also a time when your employer paid part or all of the employee's life insurance.

In our case, the employer paid part of Roy's health and life insurance. He had to pay for all the family members. We had no life insurance on the kids but a little on me. Now, very few companies pay for health or life insurance for employees *and* family members. Your best coverages on any insurance are to work with a government job. City government jobs, and even some colleges, have great benefits. Some larger companies may still cover insurance premiums to a point. At this point, we had enough to bury us if that happened since Roy retired from a city government job.

Several years later, I got to thinking about if something happened to the kids. So, I checked around and got some quotes on life insurance for them. Since the amount you pay monthly is determined by the age of the person being insured, you need to think about this sooner rather than later. I found a company that was reasonable and allowed additional life insurance amounts to be purchased after they turned fifteen and every three years after that without any medical test. So, I did that. These were also whole-life policies. Now I have them on our grandson and great-grandson. The parents will take these over in later years.

These also have borrowing power on them. Hopefully, you don't have to borrow. But we did at one point. When my daughter graduated from high school, the music department took a trip to Europe. I borrowed so I could go as a chaperone, and we had a trip of a lifetime. The interest rates are usually at a lower rate than most banks. You don't have to go through a loan process either. The policy stands for itself depending on how long you have been paying premiums and what interest it has built up. Your yearly statements should show the amount you can borrow. Remember, it can take years to build that balance, but it could be worth it. Just be aware of the borrowing amount of that policy. Some companies have a set percentage rate to charge you for a loan.

Companies are also different on when you need to start paying the loan back. Some are right after you get the check, and some are whenever you want to start making payments. Luckily, ours let us choose when to start paying the loan back and at what amount. But be aware—once you start making payments, you need to pay that each month until the loan is paid off. If you don't pay the loan back and something happens to the insured person on the policy, the policy will pay the death claim after the loan amount is taken out of the amount the beneficiary was to get.

Some people have to take out a term policy. They are cheaper for the number of years it runs for. But then, when that time is up, you no longer have that policy unless you renew and that is at a higher rate since now you are probably ten years older. Each person has to decide what they want to do and can afford at any given time.

Chapter 6

Travel Insurance

This type of insurance is if you travel a lot for work or pleasure. This insurance is also one that is fairly cheap compared to some other insurances.

I worked for a company at one point that covered all of its employees for travel. All the servicemen traveled all over the US. This was a double indemnitee's policy where the employer got half and your beneficiary got the other half in four equal, yearly installments. I don't even know if policies are still out there like that one. The company said that this way they could have the money to hire your replacement and for your family to be able to have payments for several years. That way your loved one wouldn't lose all the money if someone else tried to take over when not needed or wanted—if you know what I mean.

After I left that company, I bought an individual policy for myself. I did not remember that it only covered you until the age of seventy through the insurance company that we had car insurance under. Why it cut off, I don't know. At that age is when more people travel after retirement. So, make sure there is no age limit if you buy that or at least be aware of the age it will stop. That is probably

B. Jane Jones

one of the things I overlooked when I bought the policy. Luckily, I never had to file a claim on it. Like I said, I learned from my mistake, and I hope this helps someone not make the same ones I did.

Chapter 7

Short-Term and Long-Term Disability Insurance

This is one insurance I was never offered.

Lane had this when she worked at a university for over twenty-two years. It really helped her during different times. She had to have a knee replacement years ago with rehab that took three to six months. Now, it may only take three to six weeks at a rehab facility. Her surgery was before better options became available. So, she was able to file under short-term disability for that. Later, when she had to retire early for other health concerns, she was able to draw for a while under short-term disability insurance. The long-term disability insurance paid until about five years after her retirement. Short-term disability usually stops when long-term disability starts. This all depends on the insurance company you are with and what the illness might be.

Always be aware of what your insurance will or will not pay for. Some of the brochures they give you when you get the insurance are not always user-friendly. You would need a law degree to understand some of them, so call and talk to someone if you don't understand. I had to do that several times myself.

B. Jane Jones

This is insurance you should probably check out if you are a subcontractor, truck driver, or you are on commission only at your job. That way, if you do get sick and are out of work for a long time, you might at least get a percentage of your pay and make it until you are well and able to return to work.

Chapter 8

Long-Term Care Insurance

This is for nursing homes or special care policies.

These policies can get expensive, especially if you wait until you are older. I tried after I turned fifty and it was way too expensive, so I had to pass on it. Sometimes you can only do so much and have to hope things turn out better for you than it did for your parents or another family member.

When we had to put our dad in a nursing home, he only had Medicare insurance. They were able to get him on Medicaid also. This was over thirty years ago when it was easier to do and a lot less paperwork. When you go to check out a nursing home, you need to make sure it will be a good fit for your loved one. The one he wanted to go to was not nearly as good and it was over an hour away. The one we chose was closer to where Lane lived and worked, so she could stop on the way home and visit. Like I said earlier, he was there for around eight years. He went in not being able to take care of himself at all. They had to feed and bathe him. He was not able to walk at all. They gave him the best of care, and within a year, he was able to tend to his own needs. He was able to shuffle his feet faster than I could walk. But his health had gone down, and he was not able to live by himself again.

We had to put down three thousand dollars to get him in. This down payment was to be returned to us after Medicare and Medicaid took effect. We had to borrow the money from an uncle at the time. This usually should have only taken sixty to ninety days for processing. After that, we started asking about the refund but everyone kept avoiding us and not giving specific answers on why it was taking so long.

Come to find out, the man handling all of the down payments and such had skipped the state and was on the run. After several years, Lane happened to find out what state he went to and a phone number. How she did that I don't know, but I was glad she did. So, I started calling him. He said he was working with that state to get everything resolved. Finally, I told him I would call him every month until he got it resolved. I did, and I kept notes on dates and times, etc. about the calls. Then he finally sent us a check after five years of dealing with this and we were able to pay our uncle back. Later, I read that he went back to the state where he formally worked and was arrested. I don't remember the whole story, but I hope others were able to also get their money back.

While dad was in the nursing home, we learned a few other things you need to be aware of. Never visit your loved one on the same specific day and time. No matter how good a nursing home is, things can get overlooked and missed. Them not knowing exactly when you will drop by keeps them on their toes, so to speak. We also learned to let my sister be the good person since she lived near there and I would or could be the bad person if the need arose since I lived in another state and did not get to see him as often as I would have liked to. This came in handy in the last year or so when things really declined. You also learn which nurses or aides will help you and which ones are more apt to just give you the bare minimum answers, if any. Most of the nurses and aides were great, but you always have one or two who are not as helpful. I couldn't and didn't get angry with any of them; they were just doing their jobs, and probably a hard job at that. So that is when I would call Lane to say, "I think you need to stop by to see Dad because they are not telling me what I want to know." She would and then tell me how things looked to her.

Some Saturdays when I was in town, we would go to see Dad. We would carry our folding chairs in to visit him for the day. I can just hear the nurses and aides now, *There are those two again and they are here for the day.* Almost everyone was always nice. Dad was there for eight years, and during that time, we got to know the patients and the staff. During the last year, Dad was not able to talk much so Lane made a sign-in sheet for visitors, listing the date and time they visited and any comments they wanted to share with us. Lane put the sheet in a plastic sheet protector and put a pen it in for safekeeping. That worked out really well.

Toward the last year or so of Dad's life, we were given the option to put him on a feeding tube. They showed us other patients that were doing good with that and we finally signed. We now learned another lesson: Patients don't always come off feeding tubes, and it may have to be done again later. We let them do it again but then we both decided that was not right for the end-of-life stage. It just prolongs the suffering. We found out this was, in my opinion, a money-making thing for the nursing homes, and since this was over thirty years ago, it was probably the only option at the time. Now you have more options.

After our stepfather passed away, Mother stayed by herself. A friend of hers would come over almost every day, and they would sit and watch TV, and her friend would make lunch those days. At this point, Mother could still do some things on her own. I would go and spend a weekend with her once a month and my sister and her family would go over at different times. My niece would do the grocery shopping every few weeks for Mother. We knew her health was declining.

Then one Sunday before I left, Mother was acting a little uneasy. When I got home, I called Lane and told her I thought it was about time we started thinking about more care for Mother. It wasn't long before she called me back and said one of the neighbors had called her and said the police had found our mother wandering the street looking for her girls to come home since it was getting dark. She had scrapes and bruises on her. We never found out exactly what happened. Lane went over there and stayed until I could get there the next day.

We both sat down to start making arrangements. We got her to the doctor, and they said she had Alzheimer's.

Lane would stay with Mother so I could go check out two nursing homes. Luckily, when our mother and stepfather did their wills, they also did a dual power of attorney so that I could handle their health issues and their financial things if needed. It was needed at this point because one of the first questions a nursing home asks is to see the power of attorney (POA).

I had made appointments with both nursing homes for the next day. I first checked the one Dad had been in. They gave me a list of things that you had to have as far as paperwork before a patient could be admitted there and the cost, etc. It now costs, upfront, $10,000 to get her into either one. Then I asked about their facility for Alzheimer's patients. Theirs was a total lockdown wing. I did not get any good vibes when I went through those doors. In fact, I got a cold chill up my back. Go with your gut feeling when you are looking for care for your loved one. If you wouldn't want to be in there, then you don't want your loved one there — unless that is your only option. Each person has to make that call with whatever their situation is.

I then went to the second nursing home, had the same meeting, and was given a different paperwork list. Just so you know a few things you will need: five years of bank statements, birth certificates, marriage licenses, death certificates of spouse, and divorce papers, if any. You will also need a list of insurance policies and amounts due each month and when. See Exhibit A in the Appendix for more details that might be needed. Medicaid will tell you which of these insurance policies they will cover and what your family would have to cover. I had to take over her life insurance policy payments and I was already paying her prepay arrangements for burial through the funeral home. I was able to get Medicaid to keep paying the cancer policy for her. They said she didn't need it but I said the money would go back to them if we had to file on it. So, they paid. You don't know unless you ask. If I had to then I would have paid for it.

Nursing homes also want to know if there is a deed on the property or if they rent, etc. Mother had a home that was paid for. There are a lot of rules and regulations when you own property when you go through Medicaid. Be sure to know those rules so you don't lose more than you have to. At this point, we had to sell the house, and it took over two years. We had a lot of offers during this time. I had to deal with realtors and Medicaid, which had a hand in this. We had to get the sale approved through them. Finally, we had a cash offer and I told Medicaid this was the best we were going to get, and they approved it. I had to have some plumbing repaired so it would sell. Medicaid finally approved that I would get that money back when the sale happened and that was handled with the closing cost, etc.

The nursing home we got for Mother was an awesome place. They would hold quarterly meetings with the immediate family members and with the head nurse, social worker, activities director, head nurse's aides, and dietician. That way you got to hear from all of them in one meeting and could adjust the care your loved one was getting to better suit them. My sister and I would tell them the main two things we wanted for our mother were to be safe and happy. She was there for almost five years. Mother loved to sing the old gospel songs, so we told them whenever any group came in to be sure they took her for that, and they did. At this point, Mother did not know who we were but she could sing every word of those old gospel songs until the day she died.

One morning, I got a call from the nursing home and they told me that Mother had fallen and her breathing was bad. They put her on oxygen and called the hospice ladies in also. I called Lane and told her I needed to get some things done at work, then I would come. We decided we would go together and stay with Mother since we had a family conference scheduled for the next day anyway.

I got home to get clothes and ready to leave when I received a call from hospice that Mother was unresponsive. I left then to go to her. I was praying the whole time to keep her safe and hoping I could get there in time. Before I got to the expressway, I had this calm, awesome feeling of peace come over me, and I knew she was gone. My sister was also on the way there when she looked up, saw a star in the sky blinking brightly, and had the same feeling at the same time I did. We later found out that some of the aides and nurses were gathered around Mother's bed singing old gospel songs they knew she loved so much.

They hugged us when we got there and were so good to us. They said Mother opened her eyes and smiled as they sang, and then she was gone. What a way to go, with caring people like that around you. We were so grateful for all they did. Lane and I had been knitting prayer shawls to give to the nurses and aides there not knowing we would give them the prayer shawls the day after mother died. They also lit a candle in the hallway for her. They did that for each person who passed during their care. We invited them to come to the family visitation at the funeral home and several showed up. They were probably more family to Mother than we were because they did the day-to-day care for her for almost five years. A special thank-you to each of you who cared for her so lovingly.

This nursing home had a different way of dealing with Alzheimer's patients. They would put an ankle alarm on Mother, that way, if she went through the doors, the alarm would sound and someone would go running after her. The nurse said it usually takes a few weeks for them to adjust and then they are more comfortable with where they are. They still wear the ankle bracelet just to make sure.

The only drawback to this place was its accounting procedures. After putting down $10,000 to get her admitted, I was told that, when Medicaid finally came through, I would get the full amount back. I finally got a little over $8,000 back after six months when Medicaid had started paying from day one. They would not give us an invoice for the first six months; they would just tell us how much we owed. It takes a while before the Social Security checks go directly to them, so you have to keep paying. They said I would get the rest after everything was said and done with our mother. I would have to call every few months to try to get a statement showing how her money was being used. This went on for almost five years.

After Mother passed away, I called to see when I would get the rest of the money. They said I wouldn't get any money back. Boy, was I livid. I called the place that owned the nursing home and said I would sue to get that money. I sent a letter to the president of the nursing home company and I received a call from a lady who said they would audit the account. They did. They said they did not owe me the money. They never ever gave me a statement for the first six months there. They did say they were making drastic changes in the way the statements were done and they would then be giving statements each month. I finally told the lady that I still think they were wrong, but I had told her I would go by what they found. Getting a lawyer would have been more than that $1,000. Sometimes you just have to be glad with what you got and be glad your loved one was taken care of and move on.

Was I right or wrong? I don't know. God knows, so I just left that in his hands. If they could live with their findings, then so could I.

Just be aware, if you don't have long-term care insurance, you might be faced with losing the family home. We do what we must to get the best care our loved ones need. If you cannot afford long-term care insurance then you just need to be aware of what might happen later and try to be prepared as best as you can.

Chapter 9

Wills

I was glad we had wills drafted for us many years ago when the kids were little. When Roy passed, it was a real blessing that we had that in place. I went online to find lawyers who dealt with wills and trusts. I was able to find a great group of lawyers. They posted that in their life, they had seen family members having a rough time after their loved ones passed away. That was why they went into this field. They were awesome in helping me through this most difficult time.

I was able to do a lot of things on my own to save some money. I changed all the beneficiaries on everything we had. Now, most banks and insurance companies let you change or add beneficiaries online. Some still want you to call to make those changes. I was able to deal with some of the medical bills and dispute the payments that the insurance didn't want to pay. Some were paid for by the insurance company but not all. Remember, if you don't ask them, "How can I dispute the claim?" then they may not offer that information upfront. Ask, because there are only two answers: yes or no. If they say no, then talk to your lawyer or the insurance commissioner.

What was left in the estate had to go through some form

of probate to get settled, like credit cards, etc. Luckily, I was not listed on Roy's credit card, so I didn't have to pay that. I had my own card. Keep your cards separate if possible. If you are listed on that card, then you are held responsible. The lawyers were able to do a petition for a year of spousal support. Since we owned a house together, they had to get me exempted from paying one year of taxes on the house. Also, I needed to get papers so I would then own the house and his truck. I had never heard of the spousal support petition before, but they said it had been out there for a while. Check with your lawyer to see if you can also use that and stay out of going to full probate with the will. They still have to get notarized signatures from your immediate family members stating they have no objections to the will. If any immediate family does object, then you will probably have to go through full probate. In my new will, there is a clause that states if you object to the will and will not sign, then you are not going to get anything, even if it went to probate. Something may be better than nothing. Just be aware of this.

When my stepfather passed away, he had a will stating everything went to our mother. He had three grown children of his own. The son signed the paper agreeing to the will, but the two daughters did not sign, so we had to go to full probate. Since I was the executor, Lane and I went to probate before the judge. The lawyer for the daughters contesting the will appeared before the judge. The judge got upset because that lawyer said he was representing his clients since they could not be there. The judge dismissed him from the proceedings and said he would talk to him later. The judge then asked several questions about Mother and other things, and he also talked to our lawyer and my sister. After about an hour or so, he ruled that the will was valid, and I got a form stating this so I could then take care of Mother's vehicles and property. Since the will was contested, it cost me, out of pocket, over $1,000. Granted, that was over five years ago and before COVID. So, things were a lot cheaper than they are now.

In the process of getting the petition filed, we were also getting a new will for me. Since the pandemic began, a lot of things have changed. We did a lot of the legwork for the petition and will online, via video conference or phone. Then we went in person to sign everything. A lot of laws have also changed. The wills are now more in-depth as far as planning the "what ifs." There is now a doomsday portion where you can list people to take over if all of your immediate family has passed away.

The kids are also getting wills made. My daughter said she didn't need one, but I told her she did have stuff and shouldn't want the state or someone else getting anything. The will is for the ones left to have the legal right to deal with your belongings. So, she decided to go ahead and get her will done with the same lawyer. This way, if/when something happens to one of us, we all will know who to call to ask questions on how to go about taking care of business.

I mention this because we had an uncle die at the age of ninety-four recently. For years he said he had a will and told us his niece would take care of and get everything—except he did want his nieces and nephews to get a clock he collected and a doll our aunt had been collecting before she passed away. Well, that did not happen. The niece was in her late eighties at the time. She, nor anyone else, could remember the lawyer's name. The will was not in his safe deposit box at the bank or anywhere in the house when she went looking for it.

Weeks after my uncle passed away, a lawyer came to the house and put a lock on it until things could be settled. The problem was, someone had already come in and cleared out anything of value. Since this uncle was related through marriage to our father's sister, we never heard how this turned out.

If you lose a loved one and, now, the house is going to be sitting with no one there most of the time, you probably need to change all the locks so you know the place is secure. It is sad when you know a loved one wanted certain people to have something, like a clock or doll or just some minor thing to remember them by, but didn't get what they should have.

Make sure that more than one person knows where your will is and what lawyer you used. If you have the key, put a note in the safe deposit box to that effect and then put the note in your desk drawer where it can be found at the time needed.

Since I was waiting on a lot of paperwork to come in via mail to verify that things had been completed or changed, I signed up for the USPS postal daily email to let me know what was going to be in my mailbox that day. It is so simple to do and free. It helped me on some days to know I had to go and get the mail, or I could keep working on what I was doing and wait until maybe the next day to stop and get the mail. It's just a suggestion to make things go more smoothly.

Also, keep in mind that if you have a will in one state and move to another state, you need to do a new will for that state. Each state has different laws that need to be followed.

Chapter 10

Trusts

To help my family handle things easier, I chose to add a trust so the kids or grandkids would not have to go through any probate after I pass. Probate can get expensive and time-consuming. While talking to my lawyer, I told her what happened to my mother's house and asked if there was any way to avoid that happening to mine in case my health got bad and the family had to put me in a nursing home. The trust she told me about was a revocable trust, meaning that if I wanted to later, it could be revoked.

There is also another kind of trust called the elderly trust, which is in-depth and great for your elderly loved ones with property, valuables, their care, etc. She referred me to a specialist who handles those. That way I could make an informed decision on which way to go. I called and made an appointment with that lawyer. We spent about thirty minutes on the phone and he was great at answering all my questions. He gave me a quote to start the process and told me the few steps it would require to start. He stated that the price could go up depending on what they learned during the process, including how much you own, etc. After a weekend of thinking about the cost and time, I decided to go with the revocable trust.

Later in life, I might need to change to the elderly trust. You have to decide on this based on whatever you are going through with your family situation. Time and money also play a large part in this decision.

    I called my lawyer and told her I wanted to do the revocable trust. She emailed the information and things that needed to be done. So, when I went in to sign my new will, I was able to sign for the trust to start. I opted for it to start as soon as I signed the paperwork. Then I had to go and change all the beneficiaries to include the trust as a contingent. If you do not have the time or patience to do some of the things, lawyers can help with that. That also costs more money, but if you don't have the time or don't feel comfortable doing it yourself, let them help you. A little extra money spent may be worth your peace of mind.

Chapter 11

401(k), Annuity, and IRAs

A lot of companies offer 401(k) plans. I was lucky to work for companies over the last thirty-five years that offered this option. Most companies even match by at least 3 percent or more. If you can get into one, you should probably do it, even if it is only ten dollars or so a payday. Then, each time you get a raise, give yourself a raise in your 401(k).

A 401(k) is a retirement savings and investing plan that an employer offers. A 401(k) gives employees a tax break on money they contribute. Contributions are automatically withdrawn from the employee's paychecks and invested in funds of the employee's choosing (from a list of available offerings from that employer's plan). A 401(k) had an annual contribution limit of $20,500 in 2022 ($27,000 for those aged fifty or older). These limits may change each year so check on the web for updates and more in-depth information. Social Security may not be around when you retire years from now. Be wise with your money and let it earn money for you.

Some companies offer a loan option with their savings plans. I worked for one company that offered loans. When we bought our house, I took out a loan to pay the closing costs. This is another way to use your money without having to go and get a loan outside of your work. I had to pay the going rate of interest—at that time, it was 7 percent. I was able to run the loan for seven years with a very small payment out of each paycheck. You are actually paying yourself back the loan and the interest. All of this is building your balance back up. At that time, you could not keep contributing to the fund until after the loan was paid off but this may have changed since then.

If the company does not offer a loan option, then you probably could take a portion out and just pay the tax penalty and interest on that. I have, at one point, had to do that also. They take 20 percent out of the check you will receive for that year's taxes. When you file your taxes for that year you will have to pay a 10-percent penalty.

After 2008, when things crashed, I got to thinking about my 401(k). A few years later, I decided to check to see about an annuity to put my money into for safer keeping. Annuities are contracts sold by insurance companies that can pay regular payments to the buyer. There are four main types of annuities: fixed and variable annuities, and immediate and deferred annuities. Search the web for more details and check with your insurance company to see if they offer these and which one is right for you. Not all insurance companies have this option. Since I was over fifty-nine and a half, I could do what I wanted to with my 401(k) without having to worry about the tax penalty and interest. I pulled a good bit out and put it into an annuity. I chose the fixed immediate income annuity. This way I would get a monthly amount for the rest of my life. If I were to die before that dollar amount was paid to me then my beneficiaries would get what was left. Granted, this check was barely enough to get groceries each month. But at least I would be assured that if there was a bad crash in the economy again, I would at least eat.

Years later, when I quit my job, I looked into an IRA. I rolled over what was left in the 401(k) to my new IRA. It is sitting there earning or losing money—whatever the economy is doing right now. Because of my age, the law states that I have to take out a certain percentage each year depending on what percent the IRS states for that year. Maybe I will take that out each year at Christmas and have my Christmas gifts paid for. Again, let your money work for you.

You need to do the research to see what options are out there. Laws change all the time. What happened with my money may not happen to yours. It would be wise to review all your options each year to make sure you are doing all you can with your money and all it can be doing for you to take care of yourself in later years.

Remember, if you have an annuity, you will always have to file income tax to IRS each year, no matter what age you are.

Chapter 12

Prearrangements, Funeral or Cremation, Plots and Headstones

Before Daddy died, my sister, Lane, and I went to make arrangements since we knew it probably would not be long before he passed. The check he had gotten from a class-action lawsuit with the nursing home was put as a down payment for the burial cost. We picked out a casket and did a quick obituary for him that the funeral home kept in his file. Later, we changed some things, but at least they had that on file. We did not buy the prearrangement package at this time, we just did some of the paperwork so it would be ready when needed.

When our stepfather got lung cancer and almost died, I did prearrangements for him. Mother signed the paperwork but I paid for it each month for seven years. At some point, his son's wife tried to cash out the policy. The funeral home called me to see what was going on. They said they would not let her cash it out since Mother had signed the papers and I was the one paying for it. Luckily, they look out for the people they are taking care of. The payment plan is really like a whole life insurance policy. It goes through the insurance company and not the funeral home. On several items, you have to list a price like opening grave, flowers, etc. These are given in that day's dollar amount. When he passed away, I did have to pay a few hundred dollars extra. That was mainly because the cost of opening the grave had gone up.

When Roy passed away, the funeral home said that if we wanted the funeral on Sunday, the cemetery would charge $4,500 extra. We opted for a funeral on Monday and the policy paid for that. Since we had Roy's policy paid off by then, it had actually earned more money than what the funeral cost. We had a graveside service instead of a full chapel service which saved some money. You hear horror stories of people who have set up the policy and then have to pay a lot of money anyway. When you are setting up this policy you tell them what you will probably want at the time of your loved one's passing. It might be wise to plan bigger and then, when something happens, you can opt to change from a chapel service to a graveside service. When you do sign for this policy, it also freezes the cost of some items, like the cost of the casket. If you pay for a $3,000 casket, you will get the same value casket. If the one you picked years ago is no longer available, you will get to choose one that is comparable to that price now. Some things are not in our control. After the pandemic, things have just skyrocketed in price so I was glad ours was paid for.

When Mother passed away, I was still paying hers. She died the month before it was paid off. I did not have to make the final payment.

After Roy nearly died in an ER, I made up my mind to

go ahead and do a prearrangement with the funeral home for both of us as well. He never wanted to talk about things like this. I didn't want it to fall on the kids at a time when they may not be emotionally able to deal with it. They may not make wise decisions or may not know what we wanted. I made an appointment with the funeral home that the family has used for years. I was able to pick out the casket, guest book, and announcement for both of us. There is always a waiting period for this kind of policy to go into actual full-payment mode. Mine was for one year since I was in pretty good health at the time. Roy was not in good health so his waiting period was three years. This means that you make your monthly payments and if it's after the waiting period when you pass away, some or all of your bill may be paid. Luckily, ours had been paid off.

When we went in to verify everything when Roy passed, we were able to change some things. We did a graveside service instead of a full service at the funeral home. The price of flowers had gone up, so we used some of what we saved on the service for that. The price for the paper obituary had also gone up, and if you wanted a picture, it was $300 more so we opted not to do the picture. Since we had paid this policy off many years ago, after all the cost and everything was done, I did receive a little money from the interest that had earned on that. Every little bit helps.

When you visit the funeral home to make prearrangements, you can tell them if you want to be buried or cremated, where you want to be buried, how to handle the ashes of your loved one if they are cremated, and what newspapers you want the obituary listed in as well as the list of family members and their relationship to that person, son, daughter, wife, father, or mother, etc., what jobs you want listed, and date of birth. You list a dollar amount to go to the preacher and for flowers, opening and closing the grave, etc. Beware that the prices you are paying on this now may not be what they will be in ten or twenty years from now, or even tomorrow. The pandemic has negatively affected all these costs.

After I paid off our prearrangements, I went to a cemetery and picked out our plots. Up to this point, we had been told we could be buried in a family plot. I did not like the option of "first come, first serve" at this funeral home. I wanted to know definitively where I would be. Not that I would know at that point, but it was just a "me thing." I picked out six plots—for us, kids, and grandkids. I got those paid off with a monthly payment plan also.

After the plots were paid off, I went back and set up a payment plan for our headstones. I bought the double flat headstone. At this cemetery, you could only have a flat headstone for easier maintenance of the property. You can even buy benches with the family name on them, but I did not go this route. There are plenty of options depending on what cemetery you want to be buried in. The prices of the headstone vary by what material you want them made from and what you put on the headstone, including dates or any symbols you may want on there. I put a fisherman in a boat on Roy's side and a Bible with a cross on it on my side. Then I put the rings intertwined in the center with our wedding date. Cemeteries have numerous things to choose from, for whatever fits your taste. This is your last resting spot, and you can let it speak for you.

When your loved one passes away, you go to the funeral home to make all the final arrangements including the date of the funeral, update the obituary, and change any information that is different from what you had given previously. You also get a CD with pictures of your loved one's life that you can show during the visitation. After Lane retired, she took all of our old pictures and scanned them on the computer so that if a tornado came through or a flood, we would have those safely digitized. All the kids were given copies. So, we were able to go through Roy's pictures from early to later years and put those on the CD for the funeral home. Roy had also made a CD of three of the songs he liked to sing. He labeled it "My Last Wish." So, we had the funeral home play those songs during the visitation that day.

Chapter 13

Things to Do after Your Loved One Passes Away

1. The funeral home usually notifies Social Security about the passing of your loved one. I like to also call to make sure everything is in order. Did they send the last Social Security check to your loved one or will they be taking that back from their checking account? It depends on what the date of death was. They determine that and also send a letter to the last known address stating they had been notified that the person passed away. They do not do that if your loved one was not drawing Social Security at the time.
2. If there was a pension from a government job, you will have to notify them of the death, and they will let you know if that month's check is okay to keep or if they have to take it back from the bank account if it is being directly deposited.
3. One thing to be aware of after the passing of your loved one, and especially if you

own a home, is that you get numerous phone calls from people wanting to know if you are going to sell. Just let your answering machine or voicemail get that if you don't recognize the number. You probably do not want to deal with any of this. Wait until you can make an informed decision about anything long-term. Hopefully, your family helps with that if you need it. Or find a good lawyer that may deal in wills and trust and probate issues.

4. Go to your voter registration website in your state to let them know your loved one passed away so they can label that name as "deceased" and what date.

5. Go to the three credit bureaus to let them know about the deceased. Each one of them wants different information in a letter so they can close the account and not issue any more credit with the deceased name. See Exhibits B, C, and D in the Appendix at the end of this book.

6. If there were any medical supplies left over that can be donated, you can call each doctor to see what agencies they can recommend. I donated insulin back to the diabetes doctor's office. I donated Roy's ostomy bags to the hospital wound care

center. I donated the hospital bed to a family member who has a serious illness.
7. Your doctor's office may have a place you can take any unused medicines and dispose of them legally. Don't flush them down the toilet or put them in the trash. In Georgia, drug drop boxes are located in sheriff's and police departments across the state in 153 counties. They take your out-of-date or unused Rx and OTC drugs. Check with your local police departments to see if they offer this.
8. Notify any credit-card companies. If you are not on the card, you should not be liable for the balance. When you call, they will tell you if you are liable. If you are unsure of anything, check with your lawyer. If there is a balance you are not liable for, the lawyer can tell you how to proceed with that.
9. Go to all websites that the deceased had any accounts with and take their credit-card number off, including the lottery, health-supply places, clothes, subscriptions, etc. You would be surprised at how many that may be. If you know you will not be dealing with them again, ask them to close the account.
10. Watch their email for a while and see what

kind of emails come in. Unsubscribe to any you do not want to come through any longer. If that doesn't work, you might have to call them and tell them your loved one is deceased and to close that account.

11. You have to wait to get the death certificate before you can do a lot of things. It is usually about two weeks. If you haven't heard from the funeral home, call them and see what is happening. They can keep you posted. Be aware that some doctor's offices take a while to get that back to the funeral home. Ours did and I had to keep making phone calls for that to get settled. Finally, the funeral home called the medical examiner and they called the doctor. That got it completed.

12. The life insurance companies will need a copy of the death certificate before they can write a check to the beneficiary.

13. You will need to contact the bank. Luckily, we had a joint account, and it was switched to me with no problems. They did want a copy of the death certificate to put in the file. I also changed the beneficiaries on the accounts. If you are not listed on the bank account, the bank may put a hold on that account for a while. If you need any help with that, contact your lawyer.

14. You will need to contact the companies that the deceased had any loans with, like car loans, house loans, etc. They may also want a copy of the death certificate for their files.
15. You may need to update all of your beneficiaries on life insurance policies, bank accounts, etc. If you are thinking about doing a trust as well as a new will, you might want to wait until the trust is done. I didn't, and then I had to do all of it again. When you do change the beneficiary, put the paperwork in folders and put them in a safe place so it can be handed down to your family member. If anything happens to you, they already know what needs to be done on those and they will have all the information on hand.
16. You will probably need to update your will and/or trust too. If you don't have a will, you may want to get one, especially if you have, at this point, found what a hassle it can be if you don't have a will. Make things easier for your loved ones to deal with things when you pass away. It can get time-consuming and costly without a will, especially if you own a house or vehicle, etc.
17. You will need to file the deceased person's final tax return. I searched the web ("How

to file a final tax return for someone who has passed away"). I found the IRS Tax Tip 2022-96, June 23, 2022. It is two pages long. You can check out the website for complete information.
18. Be sure to check out irs.gov before you file a return. The laws can change each year. This, at least, gives you a starting point on what you need to do about your taxes.
19. Cancel health coverage for your loved one. Enroll in new health coverage if you or any dependents were on your loved one's policy. You generally have sixty days from the date of the person's death to enroll in new coverage.
20. Memorialize or delete your loved one's social media accounts if they had any. (You may need to contact the platform for help.)
21. Update or cancel utilities, mobile phone, internet, and TV and streaming services.
22. Prevent identity theft. Cancel their driver's license and close email accounts.
23. Forward mail and deliveries to you if your loved one lived alone.

Chapter 14

The Final Chapter (The New You)

Now that you have probably spent three months or more getting things done after your loved one passed away, it is time for you to take care of *you*.

After the first three months, I had stayed so busy with lawyers, probate, insurances, banks, etc., that I really didn't have time to think about how I was alone for the rest of my life. It is an eye-opener when you finally get to this point. Don't be afraid to seek professional help from a grief counselor—there is no shame in this. We all need a little help at times. You now want to live your life to honor your loved one and yourself.

I called my insurance company and was able to get help through them. You could go to a church or other organization that could help. My insurance company put me in touch with social services. That lady was so nice and understanding. I didn't need meals or transportation but if you do, they are there to help you. She gave me several senior centers in my county where I could go for different activities, including painting, book club, knitting, cards, exercise, firearms safety, dance, woodworking, etc. You can call them and take a tour of the facilities and see if that one is a good fit for you. You could also get with your library for book clubs or writing classes. There are so many options out there so you don't have to be alone all the time.

If you need to go into assisted living at this time, there are options out there for that as well. Also, talk to your kids and friends. They may know of other organizations you might want to check out. You may be able to volunteer somewhere to help other people. In turn, it will help you. You need to stay social to some degree. After the pandemic, I know this is harder to do, and at times you may need to stay around the house when the infection numbers are up again. But in the meantime, maybe you have made some friends and can at least talk on the phone or text each other once in a while. Be good to yourself. Everybody is different in how they handle things during a very difficult time. Whether you are young or old, there is help out there for you. You just have to reach out.

I have heard that you should not make any big, rash decisions in the first year. I can see why now. Every situation is different. Take your time and make sure it is what you want to do. Don't go by what everyone is telling you to do. You need to think clearly about the changes. Some changes will be necessary to make early on. Mine was getting the hospital bed out of the living room and donated. If you can't make the call, let one of your kids or a trusted friend who is good on the phone do that for you. Make them accountable to you for this so you are aware, but you make the final decisions.

Remember to be good to yourself and take care of yourself during this time. Get help when needed. The main thing for you to do now is enjoy whatever you decide to do. Learn to enjoy the life you have; you need to get back out there and be active. What you do now should make you feel good about yourself. If you are young and have kids, then maybe you could get more involved with volunteering at their school. Just be open to new experiences and be happy and stay as healthy and active as you can.

If you are not physically able to volunteer, you can give a financial gift to an organization so that others can do the physical part and you can feel good you are able to help in that way. Try different things until you find the one or two things that really make you feel good and happy with the *new you*.

I know this is hard because I am still trying to find the new me, but I am having fun along the way. Some days I just want to sit in my recliner and read a book or knit a prayer shawl for someone that is sick. Other days, I might try to cook something—Roy did all the cooking after his retirement. Now I am having to learn all of that again. He had everything organized the way he wanted it and now I have to figure out how I have to organize it for me. I feel like I am twelve again and learning to cook. Believe me, not everything is turning out good. I made spaghetti one night and then realized I didn't have any sauce to put on it. That is when it is good you have a lot of catsup on hand. I ordered the sauce the next day. Live and learn, laugh at your mistakes, and move on. I did make a peach cobbler that was great.

Just keep at it and stay safe and healthy.

Letter From the Author

Dear reader,

I really want to thank you for buying this book. My goal is to help you make plans so you are not caught in a situation that could be very hard to deal with. Losing a loved one is hard no matter when or how it happens. You want to be able to breathe and remember your loved one at this time, not be running all over the place trying to get answers to questions you don't even know how to ask. Even when you have made all of these arrangements, something could still come up—clothes you picked out don't fit and you have to go buy something else. That happened to us. So, I hope this book has given you some good advice so you can be prepared for the inevitable to happen. We all hope to live to be one hundred or more and to be in fairly good health, but life has its own way of turning out. Be prepared, we are all going to die.

If you have questions, seek out the great advice of a good lawyer or accountant. You could also call funeral homes to see if they can help with questions about their services. Talk to a pastor at a local church.

If this book helps you, then my prayers are

answered. Praise God. I can tell you since our arrangements had been made in advance, it was easier to sit around and remember the good times we had and to reflect on those. Not that there weren't tears shed at times, but we made it through with less hassle and worry about what we should be doing now.

Wishing you the best in life.

Take time to make informed decisions for you and your family.

God bless you,
B. Jane Jones

Appendix

Exhibit A – Example of Required Data for Nursing Home Medicaid[1]

Items listed below, if applicable to the applicant and community spouse, are necessary to determine financial eligibility. Please send photocopies of items that apply to you or your spouse. **NOTE:** This is not an all-inclusive list of verifications that may be needed. Each case is individual, and specific verification may be required during the application process.

1. Copies of Medicare, Medicaid, Social Security cards, and insurance cards.
2. Verification of the gross amount (amount before anything is taken out) of Social Security, VA, railroad, CSF checks, private pension checks, and rental income. Verification should include claim and/or identification numbers.
3. If you are a veteran or the widow of a veteran, apply for any VA benefits eligible

---

[1] This is a list of things needed to get my mother in the nursing home and to apply for Medicaid for her. The nursing home gave me this list when I went to our first meeting. They were really helpful in letting me know which things I would need for her to get admitted. However, not all pertained to her.

for. VA will provide paperwork if not eligible.
4. Copies of bank statements (any and all accounts with prospective resident's name on them and/or spouse's name) five years prior to the month of admission. The first month that the account balance exceeds $2,000 will require canceled check images.
5. Verification of CDs, IRAs, and savings bonds.
6. Verification of stocks, bonds, and mutual funds.
7. Copies of deeds to property currently owned or in which you or your spouse have an interest (heir property, life estate). Copies of original and transfer deeds to any property previously owned, sold, or transferred in the last five years.
8. Copies of trusts, mortgages, loans, and promissory notes.
9. Copies of all insurance policies: life, burial, funeral, vault, casket, cash, term and/or group, nursing home policies, health, hospital, and/or cancer policies. A copy of the card or premium notice and a copy of the payment method is needed.
10. Copies of pre-need, prepaid, and pre-arranged burial contract including an itemized list of charges.

11. Copy of power of attorney, guardianship papers, or curator papers.

The application should show the spouse's name, Social Security number, and VA claim number.

B. Jane Jones

Exhibit B – Letter to Experian Credit Bureau
Date

Experian
XXXX Street Name
City, State XXXXX

Reference: *Name of Deceased* – "Deceased. Do Not Issue Credit."

To Whom It May Concern:

1. Enclosed is a copy of my driver's license, *Relationship* of *Name of Deceased*.

2. Enclosed is a copy of *Name of Deceased*'s death certificate and driver's license.

3. Enclosed is a copy of my utility bill.

Please mark *Name of Deceased*'s file as "Deceased. Do Not Issue Credit."

My name and address are listed below:

Name
XXXX Street Name
City, State XXXXX
Please send me confirmation this has been closed.

If you need any other information, please contact me at *phone number*.

Thank you,
Name

Exhibit C – Letter to Equifax Credit Bureau
Date

Equifax Information Services LLC
XXXX Street Name
City, State XXXXX

Reference: *Name of Deceased* – "Deceased. Do Not Issue Credit."

To Whom It May Concern:

See copy of *Name of Deceased*'s death certificate, Social Security number, date of birth, and date of death.

Please mark *Name of Deceased*'s file as "Deceased. Do Not Issue Credit."

Also please notify the other two credit bureaus.

My name and address are listed below. *Relationship* of *Name of Deceased*.

Also enclosed is a copy of my driver's license. My Social Security number is XXX-XX-XXXX.

Name
XXXX Street Name
City, State XXXXX

If you need any other information, please contact me at *phone number*.

Thank you,
Name

B. Jane Jones

Exhibit D – Letter to TransUnion Credit Bureau
Date

TransUnion
XXXX Street Name
City, State XXXXX

Reference: *Name of Deceased* – "Deceased. Do Not Issue Credit."

To Whom It May Concern:

1. Enclosed is a copy of my driver's license, *Relationship* of *Name of Deceased*.

2. Enclosed is a copy of *Name of Deceased*'s death certificate.

3. Their file # is_____ *(if they give you one)*.

Please mark *Name of Deceased's* file as "Deceased. Do Not Issue Credit."

My name and address are listed below.

Name
XXXX Street Name
City, State XXXXX
Please send me confirmation this has been closed.

If you need any other information, please contact me at *phone number*.

Thank you,
Name

Acknowledgments

A special thank-you to my proofreaders: my daughter, Tracy; my son, Wesley; my sister, Lane; and my friend and former boss for over ten years, Heather.

To Joyce McDonald who also helped with finding a publisher, helpful hints for the title, and other things.

To everyone at BookLogix for making this dream come true.

A special thank-you to Jim and his staff at Carmichaels Funeral Home in Smyrna, Georgia, for all their help and support through the years.

Another special thank-you to Amanda and her staff at GA Wills, Trust & Probate Firm, LLC, in Marietta, Georgia, for helping with all the legal issues that had to be dealt with after my husband's passing.

I couldn't have done this without all of you.

Any errors in this book are solely mine.

About the Author

B. Jane Jones was born and raised in Alabama. She and her identical twin sister grew up and graduated high school in Alabama. Later, they both married and moved to Atlanta, where Jane resides today. Her two adult children live in Georgia, along with her grandson, granddaughter-in-law, and great-grandson.

Jane loves to read, knit, and crochet. Jane is now retired and she enjoys getting together with her sister, Lane, as often as they can. This is Jane's first book.

www.ingramcontent.com/pod-product-compliance
Lightning Source LLC
Chambersburg PA
CBHW071253070526
44583CB00017B/2447